BEAUTIFUL BAC
–Unique Backgrou

Sharon Kinzie

BOOK DESIGN
Michael Haselhuhn

PHOTOGRAPHY
Tom Smith

Scott PUBLICATIONS

Published by:
©1995 SCOTT PUBLICATIONS
30595 Eight Mile
Livonia, MI 48152-1798

ISBN # 0-916809-84-6
First Printing 1995

No. 3875-10-95

PRINTED IN U.S.A.

Contents & Introduction

In our travels, my husband Jeff and I have listened to the comments concerning the finishes hobbyists and professional ceramists use on their pieces. We have noted, that when an embossed piece is selected, it is almost always because of the subject matter portrayed. Usually the subject matter is self-explanatory or can be finished with very little research. What, however, do you do when you encounter the big open areas lurking behind the embossed designs— THE BACKGROUND?

There are so many easy methods and different products to use on the background areas that the variety is almost endless. We wish to encourage people to experiment with new textures, foils, and other methods to give a rich look to the background areas.

With this book, we will show multiple background techniques on a single piece to better illustrate how different each technique can make the finished piece appear.

Materials and Techniques

BRUSHES

It is very important to use the correct brushes to achieve the desired effects. Most of the projects in this book were completed with Taklon shader brushes and water-base products.

There are 3 tests that I make when selecting brushes:

1. The bristles must feel quite full, yet be soft and bouncy.

2. When I flip the bristles of a new brush back and forth across my fingers to eliminate the original sizing, the bristles should not become fluffy or bushy. The brush must retain its original knife- or chisel-edge.

3. I hold the brush up to the light to observe the individual bristles. They should be tapered away on the ends and not be cut off bluntly. If the bristles of the brush are cut, every bristle has the potential of making a streak. If the bristles taper down like a feather, when properly loaded, the brush will make nice strokes and allow easy blending.

BRUSH CARE

If you are working with a brush and it is not behaving as it should, give it a good rinse and reload it correctly. When you finish painting for the day, a good cleaning will extend brush life. Go to the sink and use shampoo to work out all trapped color from the reservoir area of the bristles. To do this hold the bristles between the thumb and forefinger of one hand and hold the handle with the other. Use pressure and a hula dance motion to move the bristles from side to side. When the brush is clean, rinse out the soap and return the bristles to their original shape. Lay the brush on a towel to dry.

FINISHES
MATTE SPRAY

No matter how I want a piece to look when finished, I usually spray it well with a matte sealer from any of the leading ceramic color companies. The reason for spraying can be explained in this way: I am sure you have at some time or other, picked up a pretty rock and thought to yourself, "If I wet this rock, I imagine the colors will become much brighter." If you spray pieces as heavily as I do, the matte spray leaves a sheen. This sheen brings out the colors and "locks in" their beauty. I often consider the piece to be finished at this point.

PORCELAIN SPRAY OVER A MATTE SPRAY

So many of our finished pieces have to be photographed and light plays havoc with highly-detailed, raised designs. Because of this, I have grown fond of somewhat duller finishes. This does not mean, however, that these finishes are unattractive. A general spray cycle begins with 2 heavy-as-you-dare coats of matte, with ample drying time between them. After the second coat has dried for about 8 hours or overnight, a coat of porcelain-type spray is applied. Take care when applying the porcelain-type spray; spray only long enough to make the surface look wet and then STOP.

TROUBLESHOOTING

If any of the surface is too heavily sprayed with porcelain-type spray and seems about to move or shift, the surface is almost guaranteed to become cloudy. By quickly respraying the area that is becoming cloudy with another coat of matte spray, you can almost always eliminate the clouding. Let the piece dry overnight, then reapply the porcelain-type spray. Porcelain-type spray over matte spray results in a flat finish that feels smooth, soft, and rich.

MATTE, PORCELAIN-TYPE SPRAY, AND POLISH

At times I like more than one texture on a piece. For example: Subject matter with a flat finish and a glossy background creates an excellent accent.

Spraying cycle—Spray two coats of matte spray as heavy as you dare over the entire piece, allowing drying time between them. The next day, carefully direct 2 sprayed coats of porcelain-type spray on the subject. You will, of course, have a little overspray on surrounding areas of the background. Don't worry about it; simply allow the piece to dry.

Polishing compound—Use a soft cloth to apply Turtle Wax polishing compound over only the background, carefully avoiding the detailed portion of the piece. Buff briskly with a clean, soft cloth just as you would when you polish a car. Reapply the polishing compound and buff as often as desired, each coat results in a finish that is smoother and glossier to the touch. The finish will be flawless with little shine and the "new car" odor will disappear in a few days.

WASHES

A wash is important to achieve depth of field, shadows, and the look of bright, bouncy colors without a heavy appearance. It is possible to use special products to thin colors, but I prefer plain water. It is free and, as I am an impatient painter, I like the drying time and also the "feel" of colors thinned with water. A common problem is that most people do not thin the colors enough when first trying to work with washes. It is better to have the color too thin and apply the wash twice in order to see it, than to have to scrub the area clean because the color is too powerful. Colors have different

continued on page 4

continued from page 3

weights and densities, so test washes by painting over newspaper print:

A thin wash will "tint" the background but not show up against the printing on the newspaper.

A medium wash colors the background and leaves a hint of color on the type.

A heavy wash colors both the paper and the type, although you should still be able to read the type through the paint.

When trying this test for wash consistency, do not overload the brush or you will not get a true test. If you are working with an oil-painted background, it may be wiser to thin the color with medium to give a more oil-like feel and allow more blending time.

PRACTICE CLOUDS

1. Choose a piece of bright blue poster board to represent a sky. Thin some White until, when used, you almost cannot see it. Using a Taklon brush at least ¼″ wide, paint 15 different lines of clouds, one under the other down the paper. Use clockwise and counterclockwise scribble strokes of random sizes at the outer edges and on the interiors of the painted clouds. Press firmly and use a scrubbing motion.

In general, clouds are billowy and lumpy in shape with rather flatfish bottoms. Some clouds have rounded ends and others taper sharply.

Once you have painted these 15 lines of clouds, do not critique your work, but set the paper aside. The next day, get out the paper and look for the best parts of each cloud. It is easy to find what we do not like, but that is unproductive. Simply look for the parts that are good and ignore the others.

Make a medium wash of White. Take a pencil and mark a location for the sun. As most right-handed people think highlighting from the right is easy and left-handed people think it is easier from the left, make a mark to indicate the sun on the side that will be better for you. Set a ruler on the sun mark and angle it toward the edges of your first cloud to show that light travels in a straight line. Treat each cloud bump in this way, but keep in mind that a really big bump could shadow the one next to it.

Use a ⅛″ brush and the medium wash of White to highlight these sunlit areas of every cloud. Also use this opportunity to change the areas of clouds of which you are not too fond. Set the paper aside.

The next day pick out parts of those clouds which are closest to the light source. Using a liner brush and full-strength White, tip, tap, and wiggle accents on the edges of the clouds. Just allow the color to flow from the brush and don't try to match any picture of clouds. You can't do anything to a painted cloud that has not already taken place in the sky overhead.

Whenever you are outside, notice the clouds; observation is your best teacher.

CLOUDS

There are three types of clouds you should know. With these 3 shapes you can make any sky.

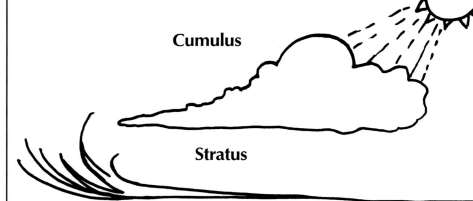

Cumulus

Stratus

Cirrus

SKIES

When working with opaque, water-base stain, I usually apply sky colors over a base coat. The base coat can be any color. Sometimes I begin with Baby Blue which gives a middle-of-the-day look. Other times I may use Wedgwood Blue for a misty, overcast effect of early or late in the day. There are also times when I use Ivory (being sure it is one without too much yellow). Whatever the color, the base coat color should be applied smoothly and allowed to dry.

As a general rule, the sky color at the horizon (where land touches sky) should be lighter to give the effect of distance. As you work upward into the sky, the color can begin to be stronger or brighter at the halfway point. If there are to be white clouds in the sky area, deeper sky color will give better contrast.

To deepen sky color, thin a stronger shade of the desired color to a thin wash. Apply this wash with a Taklon brush, making long side-to-side strokes and taking care that no strokes stop within the picture area.

Sky strokes can be applied at a slight slant, but never crisscross strokes.

If you find it hard to blend or fade out the sky color, be sure you have not overloaded the brush. Also thin the color you are using a little more.

There are many variables in blending or fading out colors as you apply them. Sometimes it requires more pressure on the brush or quicker strokes. Work back and forth and up and down while maintaining the brush-stroke angle. This will often help blend out a color. It is also helpful to add a drop of the base color to the color you are using. This makes the relationship between the base color and the sky color a little closer.

If, after trying the above suggestions, you are still having trouble blending or fading out a color, you may be able to correct the fault as follows: Beginning at the top of the sky and being sure the brush is not overloaded, brush back and forth with a wash of the base color as you work down to the trouble area. Brush gently when you reach and pass the trouble area, applying a veil of color to camouflage it.

Keep in mind that there can be some natural streaks in painted skies and you can often use them to advantage. If all else fails, place a cloud over the trouble area.

To add a little excitement to a painted sky, apply a very thin wash of a strong yellow color just over the horizon. Take care that this wash does not go too far into the blue sky area (remember yellow and blue make green!). Directly above this yellow wash, apply a very thin wash of a bright pink, streaking it back and forth and just overlapping the edge of the yellow wash.

While the yellow and pink washes can do nice things for a painted sky, you can also use other colors to equal advantage. Observe the real thing and adopt some of its effects to your paintings.

It is extremely important to vary the shape, size, and placement.

Same strokes smaller brush stonger color.

Highlights ──────▶

continued on page 6

Materials and Techniques cont.

continued from page 5

SMACK DAB TECHNIQUE

Smack dab is the name I have given to a technique for applying background colors.

Although it depends on the size of the piece, I usually choose a ¾" oval or square cut Taklon brush to apply the colors. I believe that it is important to use Taklon brushes, as they have good body and plenty of bounce. I also think that they are the only brushes that recuperate with a good cleaning.

The smack dab technique is almost always applied over a base coat.

You can smack dab with one or more colors in the brush. To load the brush, dampen it and then squeeze the water from the end. Sparingly load the bristles and tip their ends in a second color.

Use a straight up-and-down stabbing motion on a clean area of the palette to blend the colors in the brush bristles; do not overdo this step.

Aggressively using the up-and-down stabbing or pouncing motion randomly over a base coat is what constitutes smack dabbing.

You should be heavy handed enough for the bristles to fan out flat (only the metal ferrule and handle will stop you) and give wonderful explosions of color.

INTRODUCTION TO SMACK DAB

Smack dab color application is one of the most versatile and easy background color techniques. It is so simple that even a child can do it (sometimes they do it better, since, having no inhibitions, they just "do" it). The technique can provide subtle effects or make grand statements to enhance any piece, even an absolutely plain one. With this technique the background areas of all your ceramic pieces can be interesting and colorful.

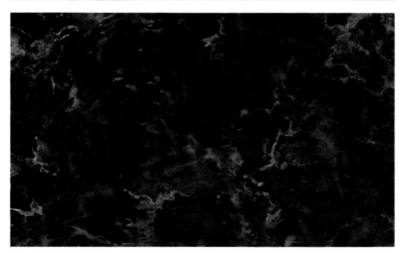

SMACK DAB COMBINATIONS

(Illus. 1)
Base coat with Ivory.

Load the brush with Medium Brown and tip it with Ivory.

Load the brush with Medium Brown and tip it with Walnut.

Variation: When the previous colors are dry, use a medium/thin wash of Walnut to paint parts of the background. Go for contrast. If the subject has a light area, make the adjacent background dark to bring it out. If the subject has dark areas, lighten the background. If the piece appears top-heavy, keep the darker colors on the bottom third of it.

(Illus. 2)
Base coat with Black.

Load in Walnut and tip in Medium Brown.

Add a third color by tipping the corner of the brush with Ivory. Note the extreme differences made by switching the base coat color when compared to the previous sample with the same smack dab colors.

(Illus. 3)

Base coat with Avocado.

Load in Avocado and tip in Turquoise.

Variations: Make a thin wash of Black and sponge or smack dab, leaving irregular untouched areas.

(Illus. 4)

Base coat with Black.

Load with only slightly-thinned Navy (this will be hard to see at first).

Load in Navy and corner load with White. Continue corner loading with more White and less Navy.

(Illus. 5)

Base coat with Hot Orange.

Load in Hot Orange and tip with Bright Red. Add a third color—Harvest Gold—on the opposite corner when working next to the main subject.

Slightly thin Black and either sponge or smack dab it on, leaving only bits of the background showing through. (Rather reminiscent of burning embers.)

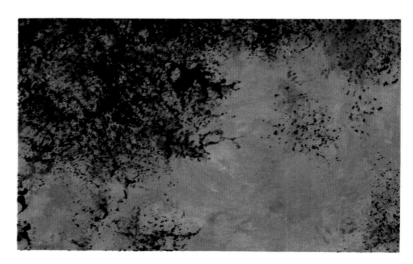

(Illus. 6)
Base coat with nonshiny opaque colors and smack dab or sponge over them with close family shades of pearl colors. For example: Base coat with Off White or Ivory and smack dab with Pale Golden Pear all over.

(Illus. 7)
Base coat with a nonfiring metallic color and smack dab with opaque or translucent stain. For example: Base coat with Gold. Smack dab with a warm Walnut and/or Black-Brown, allowing plenty of gold to show.

(Illus. 8)
Base coat with White.

Smack dab a variety of warm colors (reds, oranges, yellows, etc.) or cool ones (blues, greens, purples, etc.) all over, allowing only small clusters of White showing.

Gather several real leaves with pretty shapes. Lay the leaves, one at a time, on the piece and trace around them with a pencil.

Paint over the traced lines using a $1/8''$ or $1/4''$ shader brush and Black. As you work, paint out over background between leaves with Black. For a variation, think of a large tree's branch network—the limbs and twigs. Paint this type of pattern in Black over the background. This is a very dramatic effect that sometimes resembles the look of a stained glass window.

When you have completed the piece, spraying, not spraying, or spraying and polishing can change the look of your work.

SIDE BRUSHING

Side brushing is an easy method of applying colors to embossed and detailed designs. It is quicker and much simpler than drybrushing, but the effects are just as lovely.

Side brushing is accomplished with a chisel- or knife-edged Taklon brush and no antiquing of the piece is involved.

The technique is done as follows:

Wet the brush, then squeeze out the excess water from the ends of the bristles.

Load the brush by pressing it into a puddle of color on a palette. Use enough pressure so the brush fans out and accepts color throughout the bristles. Turn the brush over and repeat the loading process. Press one side and then the other of the loaded brush up and down on a clean area of the palette to distribute the color evenly.

Fold a paper towel in half and anchor it with the water bowl. Lay the bristles of the loaded brush flat on this towel and pull it twice the length of the bristles. Turn the brush over on the same spot and pull it again twice the length of the bristles. Repeat until the paper towel begins to rise a bit with the brush or begins to feel sticky. (If this does not happen, you may have left too much water in the brush before loading it with color, or you may have pushed so hard you have "glued" the paper to the table.) Properly loaded and conditioned on the towel, the brush will contain ample color for painting.

Each time you load the brush with the same color, return to the same spot on the paper towel to "dress" the brush.

Do not apply the color to the piece with the ends of the brush bristles. Use the brush about halfway up on the flat side, hence the term side brushing.

Do not brush on the color, but lock your wrist and pull the brush with your arm. Angle the piece until the brush hand is comfortable and do not allow the brush bristles to bend.

Side brush over a dry base color and the raised details of the design will draw the color from the brush. After side brushing for a few minutes, check to see the results. If it takes more than 3 brushstrokes to achieve a bright color in any one area, or if the color looks smoky, you may still have too much water in the brush or you have removed too much color on the paper towel. If you color not only the raised details but also the crevices, check the brush angle—it should be lying almost parallel to the surface being decorated with the brush ferrule almost hitting the piece. Try to always brush across raised details.

The term **dust** is applied to a very gentle side brush application of color.

Tickle is a term used for a hint of color and an even lighter handed application. This can be used in areas where the brush cannot be held parallel to the surface. Work nearer the brush bristle tips and have them slightly pointed downward toward the surface of the piece. Carefully move the brush from side to side over the raised details. Use this method only when necessary and do not make a habit of using this brush angle. It is very wearing on the brush bristles and they will fluff out or roll up.

Slide means to apply color by laying the flat side of the brush on the piece and pulling it down in the direction of the raised details such as on a feather quill.

CRACKED, CRAZED, OR VEINED LOOK

These effects are achieved by applying color over a dry background. You can use brushes in a variety of sizes, depending on the desired width of line or size of pattern.

Step 1—Load a large brush with water and use it to dampen small areas at time.

Step 2—To achieve a fine line or to help distort lines, use water to thin the color with which you are working. The object is to achieve variety in an assortment of shapes, line widths, and placement. While a line is still wet, I sometimes shove it from side to side or add more water; the additional water often makes a dribble that I control by guiding it with a wet liner brush. Occasionally, extra water will lighten the color and make a broad area. You can distort the lines by angling the painting surface, or by blowing on it through a straw. Sometimes I use a clean, damp brush to take color from a broad area that is still wet to leave a hollow or empty ring effect.

Step 3—Attend to one or two lines at a time. When the areas are dry, you can enhance the edges of the lines with an outline or make the lines look more intricate.

I like to think of a map of roads or a river network while developing this portion of the technique. Lightning shapes or spider webs are also good shapes to imitate.

Step 4—If you wish the background under the lines to be a shade or two darker, or warmer in tone, allow the lines to dry. Make a thin wash of Black or a darker tone of the previous color and paint it over the area. A true wash will only tint underlying color and will not eliminate all of your hard work.

continued on page 10

Materials and Techniques cont.

continued from page 9

Step 5—If you would like to have very fine vein lines, try applying the color with a crow quill pen. Crow quill pens are available at office supply or artist's supply shops where metallic gold and other colors of inks can also be found. Fine work of this type is especially nice on fairy or butterfly wings.

A trip to a tile store can furnish ideas for this type of work (individual tiles can often be purchased and retained for reference). Illustrations in books on semi-precious rocks and stones are another source of ideas.

LEAF PRINTING

Work of this type is beautiful over any combination of smack dab colors. Choose a contrasting color for the leaf silhouettes, sometimes using it in combination with metallics or with pearl colors.

Go scouting around your yard or a wooded area and look for leaves of different shapes and sizes. (No poison ivy or sumac please!) If you are not planning to immediately work with the leaves, put them in a plastic bag with a wet sponge to keep them fresh.

Layer your work area with newspapers. Select at least 3 colors for a smack dab background (Ivory, Medium Brown, and Walnut were used for the pictured piece). Cut some newspaper into 6" squares. Have available a ¾" Taklon shader brush.

Step 1—Use a clean brush to base coat the item to be decorated with Ivory.

Step 2—Thin separate amounts of Medium Brown and Walnut into washes. Sparingly load the ¾" brush with Medium Brown and tip with Walnut.

Smack dab the piece, beginning at the bottom and working upward at random over the entire surface. Try to achieve a vague, but interesting mottled background. Temporarily set the piece aside.

Step 3—Practice leaf printing as outlined before trying it on the piece. One side of a leaf may have a nicer pattern than the other and testing is the only way to find out.

Heavily coat an area of the newspaper with Black, making it about twice the size of the selected leaf. Quickly paint one side of the leaf as evenly as possible. Set the painted side of the leaf on the sticky painted area of the newspaper. Gently tap your fingers all over the leaf. Lift the leaf by its stem, then set it back in the same place. Repeat this lifting and replacing a few more times to remove any excess color. Set the prepared leaf, paint side down, in a clean spot on the newspaper, taking care not to slide or "scoot" the leaf. Hold the leaf in place and cover it with a square of newspaper (the paper will allow you to press on the leaf without tearing it). Slide your fingers over the paper-covered leaf. Without moving the leaf, carefully lift the paper square. Peek under the leaf as you slowly peel it up. If there are any missed areas, put the leaf back and rub over it to complete the impression. Test several leaves in this way to see which are the best sides and which leaves have the nicest shapes.

Step 4—Beginning with the largest of the selected leaves, set it on the prepared piece over the dry smack dab background. Imprint the leaf shape and vein pattern on the piece. Continue to apply prints of the other leaves to make an attractive pattern. (I try to make a pattern look as though I had a bouquet of leaves fanning out from a central point.)

Step 5—Allow the completed leaf prints to dry. Make a very thin wash of Walnut and use it to tint some of the leaf silhouettes.

Step 6—Sign the piece. Spray the piece with 2 heavy-as-you-dare coats of matte sealer, allowing each coat to dry well. Allow the piece to dry for about 24 hours, then polish it as directed in the Matte, Porcelain-type Spray, and Polish section.

Small Plain Rock

Serpentine Technique
(Semi-precious stone)

On some pieces the background can be so outstanding that nothing more is needed. The **serpentine technique** can provide just such a background, and can be carried out in several family color groups over a black base color. Some family color groups are: Burnt Orange, Walnut, Medium Brown, and Ivory; or Navy, Bright Blue, Baby Blue, and White.

I use this technique on the background areas of several pieces such as the small rock which can be used as is or made into a clock as pictured.

Step 1—If you wish to make the greenware rock into a clock, cast the mold and place the greenware in a plastic bag to keep it damp until you are ready to begin work. If you purchase the greenware, request that it be kept damp for you.

Step 2—Carefully; so that you do not distort the damp greenware, gently hold the clockworks in the desired location and lightly sketch around it with a pencil. Using a cleaning tool or a sharp knife, carefully cut through the greenware inside the pencil line. Remove and discard the round cutout portion. Allow the greenware to dry.

Gently set the clockworks into the hole in the greenware rock to check the fit. The clock should fit a little loosely to allow for shrinkage that will take place when the greenware is fired. Adjust the opening as necessary.

Step 3—Clean the greenware in the usual manner, then fire the piece to cone 05.

Step 4—Base coat the bisque rock with Black.

Step 5—Collect all the old, beat-up, toothy-looking brushes that you have neglected to throw away.

Look at the photo and notice the angles, varied lengths, and widths of the brushstrokes.

Thin some Dark Green with water to a medium wash. Sparsely load a worn ¾" brush with the thinned color and streak it on the rock from the 10 o'clock to the 5 o'clock position. Do not try to cover all of the Black base color and do not go back over any brushstrokes. (These initial brushstrokes establish the angle that you should try to maintain throughout the painting.)

Step 6—Add a drop of White to the Dark Green wash, making sure the mixture is still transparent. Add streaks of this color, switching brushes and brush sizes for more interesting streaks. Occasionally overlap a previous streak.

Step 7—Thin the wash again so it will just show. Load a ragged ¼" brush and, using short, side-to-side, shaky strokes, trail the brush to produce another type of streak. Add only a few of these strokes to the piece.

Continue as directed above, using Avocado and Chiffon Green.

Step 8—Look again at the photo and notice that some lines seem to be cracked. To achieve this effect, use a liner brush and a slightly-thinned solution of Black. Also add an occasional cluster of dots for the look of natural pitting.

As you work on the piece, keep in mind that there should be variety in the shapes of the color lines and in the Black spaces between them.

Step 9—At this point the serpentine effect is complete. If you wish to add further decoration as directed in the following chapter, "Tiger in the Wild Roses," do not spray the piece. If you like the piece as it is, spray with 2 coats of matte sealer and polish as directed in the section on Finishes.

If the piece is to be a clock, install the clockworks.

Kinzie Mold K3

A Tiger in the Wild Roses

This design is to be applied over a piece with a **serpentine technique** background.

Step 1—Clean the greenware, then fire it to cone 04.

Step 2—Apply a serpentine technique background as outlined in the previous chapter. Do not spray the piece.

Step 3—Make a copy of the design and transfer it to the piece with Yellow or Blue Saral Transfer Paper®, pressing firmly with a ballpoint pen. (This type of transfer paper can be obtained from art supply stores.) Remove any unwanted traced lines with a clean pencil eraser.

Step 4—To prevent the background color from bleeding through the design colors, apply 2 coats of White to the flower petals, bud, and butterfly wings. Take care that you do not loose the separation between the butterfly wings when applying the White.

Step 5—Make a thin wash of Bright Pink. Lightly tint the flower petals with this wash by pulling color outward from the flower center. Also apply this color to the bud. Highlight each petal about 2/3 of the way from the center to make them look curved, using a 1/8″ shader

brush and shaky left-to-right strokes. Deepen the color near the flower center with a thin wash of Magenta. Add a touch of the same color to the buds.

Step 6—Fill in between the flowers with a heavy wash of Black, at the same time using this color to alter flower shapes as necessary. Paint shadows under the flowers.

Step 7—Use the tip of a small brush handle to dot the flower centers with Burnt Orange. Add a few dots of Harvest Gold on top of the Burnt Orange ones.

Step 8—Paint the leaves as follows: Paint one side of each leaf with a 1/8″ Taklon shader brush and Avocado. Start at the tip of the leaf and stroke in toward the center vein. Work down to the stem end, allowing some background to show in the center. Repeat for the other side of each leaf. Highlight the leaves with Lime. Use the same types of strokes, but making them much shorter. Use Lime on the foremost edges of

some leaves and on the tips of some large leaves.

Step 9—Load a liner brush with Avocado and side load it with Burnt Orange. With the brush loaded in this way and reloading as required, paint in the stems. Follow the traced lines and slightly roll the brush as you draw it along.

Step 10—Use the 1/8″ shader brush and a heavy wash of Black to paint the leaf and branch shadows. Make "holes" in the leaves for a natural look by adding irregular spots of Black.

Step 11—Make a very thin wash of Harvest Gold. Lightly load the brush with this wash and paint the butterfly wings with strokes that sweep outward from the body. Thin a bit of Burnt Orange to an extremely thin wash and tint about halfway up each wing with the same types of strokes.

Step 12—Use a thin wash of Black for the fine vein lines on the butterfly wings. Outline a large oval on each wing near the body, then add lines arcing outward from the body. Paint 2 fine lines for the butterfly's antennae and also add vein lines on the leaves. Add the butterfly's "tiger" stripes.

Step 13—Block in the borders of the butterfly's wings with Black and outline each wing with fine lines of the same color. Allow the piece to dry, then use a brush handle to add dots of Harvest Gold in the Black border areas.

Step 14—Paint the butterfly's body Lime. Load the liner brush with a wash of Black and paint lines to divide the body into segments.

Step 15—Spray the piece with 2 coats of matte sealer and allow to dry, then polish as directed in the section on finishes.

Kinzie Mold K3

Twin Fawn Frame

POURING TECHNIQUE
(Frame and picture, pour as one piece)

Step 1—Pour the mold and when the greenware is the correct thickness, drain out the excess slip. Let the mold stand for 2 to 3 hours to allow the greenware to set up.

Step 2—Prepare a support for the back of the picture area. Cut the support a little smaller than the pour gate. Set the support in place. Remove the waste around the pour gate and lift off the back of the mold. Lay a flat board over the wet greenware. Hold the board firmly in place as you carefully turn the mold over. Carefully remove the front section of the mold and allow the greenware to dry.

PAINTING TECHNIQUE
Step 1—Clean and fire the greenware.

Step 2—Base coat the sky area with Ivory, using a ¾" Taklon brush. Do not be concerned if the sky color overlaps the embossed design, just be sure the color is not heavy enough to clog the details.

Step 3—Place quarter-size puddles of Chiffon Green and Turquoise in separate spots on the palette. Sparingly load the ¾" brush with Ivory and tip it with Chiffon Green. Use an up-and-down motion on the palette to blend the colors. Using the smack-dab technique, apply the colors at random over the sky area. Occasionally tip the brush with Turquoise and repeat the smack-dab application.

Step 4—Use a worn out square shader brush and a medium wash of Avocado to stipple in dangling branches in the right corner behind the trees.

Step 5—Base coat all remaining areas with Black. Also stipple Black between the background leaves and flowers (see the photo).

Step 6—Side brush the ground, the old stump, and the fawns with Walnut.

Step 7—Side brush the trees at the left with 1 or 2 coats of Ivory. Start at the bottom and pull upward, leaving the color slightly darker at the sides of the trunks and lighter in the centers. Side brush Ivory on the wood area of the stump and on the areas without bark.

Step 8—Side brush highlights on some dead leaves, the fawns, and the bark. Also side brush this color here and there on the ground. Thin Medium Brown to a medium wash and randomly tint wood parts of the stump, the roots, and areas without bark. Apply patches of the Medium Brown wash to the trees. Tint the fungi on the stump with the same color.

Step 9—Heavily side brush the leaves behind the fawns with Avocado, keeping the color out of the crevices. Stipple the Black areas of the leaves with a little Avocado. Highlight some parts of the leaves with Harvest Gold and other parts with Lime, to achieve contrast. Make some of the foreground leaves Brown.

Step 10—Referring to the photo, paint some flowers Harvest Gold and the others White. Use Harvest Gold for centers of the white flowers and Walnut for the centers of the yellow ones. Stipple all centers with Burnt Orange.

Step 11—Make a medium wash of Harvest Gold and highlight the fawns wherever you think the sun would strike them, areas such as tops of the heads, backs of the ears, tops of the cheeks, tops of the legs, and on the backs.

Step 12—Heavily side brush the inside of the ears with White. Make thin washes of Bright Pink and Harvest Gold. Tint inside the ears with the

Bright pink wash, then apply the Harvest Gold over that. Allow the piece to dry.

Make a medium to thin wash of Burnt Orange and tint all brown areas of the fawns' fur to give them a slight glow. Allow the piece to dry. Also tint the yellow flowers near their centers.

Sparingly use the above washes at random over the breaks in the trees, inside the stump, and on the areas of the stump with no bark.

Step 13—Set in the shadows with 2 separate very thin washes: Purple and Navy. Use Purple on the left sides of the trees and low in the center crack inside the stump. Use the Navy wash for cast shadows of the fawns on the stump. Tint the bottom of the trees at an angle to indicate the cast shadow of the stump on them. Allow the piece to dry.

Step 14—Gently side brush inside the stump with Ivory to bring out the details. Paint the tops of the fungi Medium Brown and tint them with a heavy wash of Walnut.

Step 15—Paint the spots on the fawns with White and a detail or liner brush, making tiny short strokes in the direction of the fur texture. Trim along the tail, the rump (stopping at the dent), the fine hairs on the back leg, above the noses, along the bottoms of the cheeks, the eye patches, and the muzzles. Lightly side brush White over the pinkish areas inside the ears to accent the fur texture.

Step 16—Paint ragged patterns of Black inside the ears as shown in the photo. Add a narrow Black border to the white tail trim. Apply Black to the hooves and the eyes. Be sure all crevices are Black, touching up if necessary. Use a medium wash of Walnut for the irises of the eyes and highlight each with a touch of White.

Kinzie Mold KF3

PAINTING THE FRAME

Step 1—Paint the frame with a mixture of equal parts of Harvest Gold and Medium Brown. Use a ¾'' brush and a medium wash of Walnut to sketch in the wood grain. Make the grain with long, jagged ''V'' shapes or with long, jagged lines. Paint a Black band on the second raised area from the picture. Add extremely fine lines of Black for the corner joints.

Allow the piece to dry, then spray it with matte sealer and allow to dry overnight.

Step 2—Antique the frame with Black-Brown translucent stain. Wipe the wet surface with a soft cloth, allowing the wiping streaks to show.

Step 3—If desired, purchase some self-sticking metallic gold pin striping from an automotive shop and adhere it to the inner border of the frame.

Step 4—For an exceptional touch of realism, spray a soft cloth with Johnson's Lemon Pledge® and buff the frame. Friends will think they are feeling and touching real wood!

Indian Girl and Pony

Step 1—Clean the greenware, making sure the lid fits the box correctly.

Fire the box with the lid in place to cone 04.

Step 2—Pour glaze the insides of the box and lid with Antique Brown glaze. Use a brush to bring the glaze up and over the lips of the box and the lid.

Allow the pieces to dry, then fire them to cone 05.

Step 3—Using Ivory opaque stain, base coat the bisque areas of the box and, avoiding the girl and pony, also base coat the bisque areas of the lid.

Step 4—Place 2 small puddles of Medium Brown stain in separate spots on the palette. Thin one puddle of stain with clean water to a thin wash. Select a sponge with a fine hole pattern and dampen it in clean water. Squeeze the sponge as dry as possible, then lightly touch it to the Medium Brown wash. Tap the sponge on a dry area of the palette, then gently pat around the very edge of the lid to achieve a very pale color pattern. Continue in the same way to work into the picture area with overlapping sponge impressions. Add a few drops of full-strength Medium Brown to the wash. Use this slightly darker color to make a ¼"-wide border around the edge of the lid.

Step 5—Working with the same colors as in the previous step, sponge from the top down and from the bottom up on the sides of the box, leaving an area of the base color showing in the center. Referring to the photo, sketch in mountains around the side of the box. Use a ¼" brush to paint the mountains Medium Brown and shade them with a very thin wash of Walnut.

Step 6—Base coat the pony with Black.

Step 7—Determine which areas of the pony are to be white and side brush them with White. Side brush all remaining areas of the pony with Walnut. Assuming that the sun is coming from the left rear, highlight with a little Burnt Orange any Walnut areas you think the sun would strike.

Step 8—Paint the pony's eye and hoof Black. Use some thinned Black to shadow the nostril and to outline the legs.

Step 9—Base coat the girl's skin areas with Native Flesh and allow them to dry. Coat the skin area with a very thin wash of Burnt Orange, taking care not to leave any streaks. Complete the skin areas with thin washes of Walnut, being sure to allow drying time between them.

Step 10—Place a pea-size drop of Bright Red on the palette. Use the "No Fail" cheek technique to blush the cheeks and other areas as follows:

Fold a paper towel and anchor it with the water bowl. Dip your fingers into the water bowl. Hold your hand above the bowl until the water stops dripping from your fingers. Touch your fingers to the paper towel. Dampen and sparsely load a ¼" worn shader brush with the Bright Red. Brush all the color from the brush on a corner of the paper towel. Test the brush against your palm; if any color shows, brush again on the towel. When color no longer shows on your palm, tap both sides of the brush on the area of the towel dampened by your fingers. Using the brush with a light touch and an action you might use with a feather duster, blush the girl's cheeks, temples, tops of her shoulders, throat, between her fingers, bottoms of arm and elbow, knees, and both sides of leg crease.

Step 11—Mix a little Walnut into the Bright Red on the palette. Thin this mixture to a medium wash and apply to the lips. Add the lash lines, brows, and mouth separation line with a slightly-thinned mixture of Walnut and Black.

Step 12—Base coat the dress and feathers with Ivory. Darken the creases, folds, and outline the fringe areas with a medium wash of the Walnut-Black mixture. Set in the larger body shadows such as her back and waist contour, under the bust, front and stomach, bottom of sleeve and the lap area with a thin wash of Medium Brown.

Step 13—Paint the moccasin Medium Brown. Base coat the hair, dress trim, and thong in her hand with Black. Accent a few strands of hair with Walnut. Use a thin wash of Walnut to accent the feathers, applying the color inward from the outer edges. Use the same color to add a hint of shadow under the figures and the small stones. Use a wash of Black to strengthen the shadows.

Step 14—Paint the moccasin lacing Turquoise. Use a toothpick or a stylus to add "beads" with Turquoise and White. Slightly thin some Black and outline the opening of the moccasin and the strap. Outline all crevices on the pony and girl where necessary. Apply narrow edges to the feather and outline the quills.

Step 15—Side brush White over all White areas and the feathers to brighten them. Bring out details on the pony if necessary by applying a medium wash of Black and immediately wiping it back with a dampened soft cloth.

Step 16—Allow the box and lid to dry, then spray them with 2 coats of matte sealer. Let the pieces dry overnight, then spray them again; this time with porcelain-type sealer.

Kinzie Mold K1 (Box) K1F (Lid)

Baby Bear and the Honey Tree

Step 1—Clean the greenware. If desired, cut a "knothole" in the side of the tree.

Fire the greenware to cone 05.

Step 2—Base coat the entire piece with Ivory. Prepare a very thin wash of Medium Brown. Wet a sponge and squeeze it dry. Choose an area of the sponge with an interesting hole pattern and load it with the thinned color. Press the sponge up and down on the palette. Using a light, patting motion apply color to the sides and all rock areas of the piece (if the color is thin enough, you should barely be able to see it; if necessary, thin the wash a little more).

Add a few drops of Medium Brown to the wash on the palette. Sponge this color on the sides of the piece and include about ¼" all around the edge of the picture area.

Make a thin wash of Walnut and sponge it on to darken the edge and the picture area about ¼" up from the bottom.

Step 3—Paint all leafy areas Black and allow them to dry. Drybrush or side brush Avocado on the leaves, then highlight the ends of them with Lime.

Step 4—Use a liner brush and a thin wash of Harvest Gold to streak up and down the center tree. Ignoring the bark areas, shadow the sides of the tree and the bottoms of the branches with a medium wash of Medium Brown. Use the same color to tint the ground up to the foliage. Apply this wash to the 2 background trees.

Step 5—Avoiding the muzzle, tint the entire bear with a medium wash of Medium Brown. Shadow the border of the bear with a thin wash of Walnut, applying the strokes in the direction the fur would grow. Darken the eye areas and the center part of the fur on the face.

Step 6—Use a detail brush and Black to dot in the eyes and to shadow the ears.

Step 7—Base coat the rough bark of the tree with Black. Side brush or drybrush the bark with Walnut. Apply Burnt Orange to the bark in a hit-or-miss fashion. Tint the bear's cheek with a thin wash of Burnt Orange.

Step 8—Cover the broken top part of the tree with a thin wash of Harvest Gold and allow it to dry. Using a medium wash of Medium Brown, paint upward in the broken area, leaving a ragged edge near the top. Add a thin wash of Walnut about halfway up the same area. Set a medium wash of Black in at the bottom of the broken area. Paint the knothole Black. Accent the bear with a thin wash of Black, applying fine lines and including the nose and muzzle. Outline the tree and bark with a medium wash of Black.

Step 9—Block in the rocks with Gray and highlight their right sides with Ivory. Underline the rocks with fine lines of Black, pulling the color out to the left.

Step 10—Shade the side of the tree and under the branches with a thin wash of Purple. Allow the piece to dry.

Step 11—Spray the piece with 2 heavy coats of matte sealer, allowing drying time between coats. Allow the piece to dry overnight, then spray it with porcelain-type sealer for an extra smooth finish.

Kinzie Mold K3E Rock

Deer on Rock Ledge

Step 1—Clean the greenware, then fire the piece to cone 05.

Step 2—Carefully avoiding the deer, trees, and foreground ledge, base coat all remaining areas of the bisque piece with Baby Blue.

Step 3—Refer to the photo and note that the sky colors are at a slight angle. Lighten the sky area over the mountains with long, sweeping strokes of Ivory. Apply these strokes from the tall mountain, taking them to the left at a low angle. Keep the brush moist as you load it with color and allow a few vague streaks of blue to show.

Step 4—Thin some Harvest Gold with water to an extremely thin wash. Maintaining the same angle as in the previous step, tint the area over the mountains. Repeat this procedure with a thin wash of Pink at the top of the Harvest Gold.

Step 5—Make a very thin wash of Purple and tint a ¼″ streak above the Ivory area. Make a narrow upward line with long, feathery wisps at the end.

Prepare a wash of White. Using small shader brushes, scrub on a narrow row of clouds, working as described in the section on painting clouds.

Step 6—Shadow the distant mountains to the left with a wash of Purple. Add some "scribble" strokes with a medium wash of Wedgwood Blue.

Step 7—Tint the next 2 rows of mountains with a very thin wash of Cinnamon, allowing the color to puddle at random. Strengthen the Cinnamon on the palette to a medium wash and pat this mixture on the mountains to brighten their colors.

Step 8—Pat a very thin wash of Purple over the Cinnamon. "Scribble" the Purple wash over the farthest mountains. Use a ¼″ shader brush and the same color to add tints to the mountain behind the pine trees.

Step 9—Heavily side brush full strength Baby Blue over the farthest mountain to bring out its detail and lightly over the other mountains.

Step 10—Base coat the deer, ledge, rocks, and all trees with Black.

Step 11—Side brush Walnut on all tree trunks and on the deer, avoiding the insides of its ears, the rump, tail, muzzle, and cheek. "Scrub" off the color remaining on the brush on random areas of the rocks and the ledge; repeat this scrubbing procedure in Steps 12 through 16.

Step 12—Brighten the deer's back, hips, shoulder area, and throat with Medium Brown. Highlight the Medium Brown areas by "dusting" them with a medium wash of Harvest Gold. Warm the lower tummy, lower throat front, back leg, and top of the head with a thin wash of Burnt Orange. Highlight to the left of the 2 largest trees with a medium wash of Burnt Orange.

Step 13—Use Avocado for the pine needles and highlight them with Harvest Gold.

Step 14—Paint White inside the deer's ears, around both eyes, on the muzzle, throat patch, lower breast, stomach, rump, tail, and inside sides and back of front legs.

Step 15—Mix a little Medium Brown into Ivory and apply to the areas of the 2 trees where the bark is missing. Use the same mixture for the deer's antlers, lightening or darkening it to contrast with the sky.

Step 16—Use a medium wash of Pink in the center of the ears. Apply a very thin wash of Harvest Gold over the Pink.

Step 17—Side brush Wedgwood Blue over the ledge and the rocks, keeping this color out of the crevices. Bring up the details in these areas by "dusting" them with White.

Step 18—Paint a small plant between the ledge and the rocks, using Avocado for the leaves and several dots of Burnt Orange to represent blossoms or berries.

Step 19—Paint the tip of the deer's tail, the eyes, and nose Black. Load a liner brush with a heavy wash of Black and paint lines to separate the rocks. Soften these lines with a small shader brush. Indicate the separations in the deer's legs, the shadow under the neck, and between the legs and tail in the same way.

Step 20—The painting can be considered finished at this point. However, before spraying the piece with sealer, you might like to add some interest to the back of the rock. If so, add a line for Wedgwood Blue pine trees across the back, then paint from the trees down to the bottom with the same color (see the photo). Also brush Wedgwood Blue inward from the edges of the piece above the pine trees.

Step 21—Allow the piece to dry, then spray it with 2 coats of matte sealer, allowing drying time between coats. Let the piece stand overnight, then spray it with porcelain-type sealer for a beautiful look and a smooth finish.

Kinzie Mold KR6

Eagle Painting Instructions

Step 1—Base coat the eagle's body, legs, feet, and wings with Black. Base coat the tail, neck, and head with Wedgwood Blue. (I don't like to use Black under areas that are to be finished with light colors. Base coating in this way keeps white areas cleaner looking and makes them easier to do.)

Step 2—Load a ½" Taklon shader brush with Walnut and side brush all Black areas, keeping this color out of the crevices. Use a smaller brush to paint the feet with the same color.

Step 3—Side brush Burnt Orange over the Walnut areas, once again avoiding the crevices that divide the rows of feathers. Apply this color more heavily on the ends of the 2nd and 3rd rows of feathers. Cover all of the body but about ¼" around the edge with Burnt Orange. Make the tongue the same color.

Step 4—Use Harvest Gold on the center feathers of the leg, on a center oval of the breast area, on the shoulder tops, on the 2nd and 3rd rows of feathers on the left wing, and across the center quill of each long flight feather.

Step 5—Paint the feet heavily with Harvest Gold, avoiding the crevices. Also use this color on the beak and nostril area. Tip the end of the upper mandible with a light mixture of White and Harvest Gold. Dab a bit of this mixture at random over the nostril area.

Step 6—Use a ¼" shader brush loaded with White to paint inward from the ends of the tail feathers. Apply the color so it is very bright and allow it to fade off about halfway up the tail. Let the base color show in the detail crevices and do not have a definite stopping line. Coat the same areas again to be sure they are very White.

Apply White to the head, allowing the base color to show in a few lines (do not allow too many lines of base color to show, or the area will look like fur rather than feathers).

Step 7—Paint the eye Black with a narrow ring of Harvest Gold at the bottom. Paint the 4 talons on each foot Black.

Step 8—Add enough water to some Black to make a thin wash. Use this wash to shadow the inside of the beak and for a fine line around the entire beak and the tongue. Make the edges of the nostril ragged and not as dark as the eye.

Use a thin wash of Walnut to deepen the shadows in the crevices that make the scale pattern on the legs and feet. Also use a fine line of this color under the nostril area.

Step 9—Make a thin wash of Wedgwood Blue. Use a ¼" brush and this wash to shadow the white feathers under the throat and in the crevice at the top of the eye. Pull this wash out from the body about half the length of the tail. Deepen some of these shadow areas with a very thin wash of Purple, pulling it out about half the length of the blue shading. Shadow here and there on the white head feathers with Purple. Allow the piece to dry and check to see if the wash colors are too bright. If they are, tone them down by side brushing them with White.

Step 10—If you have completed the side brushing properly, you can eliminate this step. However, read it through just to be sure your painting is as it should be.

Check to see that all feather separations are distinct. In the brown areas, you can enhance the piece by adding a heavy wash of Black in the division lines. In the tail, the divisions should be Wedgwood Blue and/or Purple. If they are not, add them with a liner brush. Be sure the head feathers have a vague, soft look.

Screaming Eagle Rock

Step 1—Clean the greenware, then fire the piece to cone 04.

Step 2—Base coat the entire bisque piece with Ivory, using a ¾" Taklon brush.

Step 3—Mix equal parts of White and Suntan. Smack dab this mixture up against the wing and body of the eagle, leaving ragged outer edges around the area. Continue to smack dab the color at random over the remaining background areas.

Step 4—Dampen a sponge, then squeeze it as dry as possible. Thin some Medium Brown with water. Set the sponge into this thinned color, then press it on a clean area of the palette once or twice to distribute the color on the sponge. Begin tapping the sponge at the edges of the rock. As these areas are covered, begin to apply the color more lightly into the picture area, taking care not to go over the wing feathers (see the photo). Apply a broader band of the color at the bottom of the piece, bringing it quite close to the eagle's tail.

Bring the same color around the edges of the piece to the back, leaving the top center relatively clear of color.

Step 5—Thin some Walnut to thin wash. Sponge this color over the same areas of the preceding step, keeping it a little farther from the picture area.

Step 6—Use a straight edge and a pencil to lightly sketch in the 3 lines to represent trees. Using a small shader brush and Black, go over these lines, making each a different width.

Lightly pencil in a few branches as shown in the photo. Make the branches wiggly and knobby and be sure they are wider at the tree and become narrow as they tilt downward.

Step 7—Place small amounts of Walnut, Medium Brown, Wedgwood Blue, and Black on the palette. Select areas of the trees to be free of bark and apply Ivory to them with a small brush. Make a thin wash of Medium Brown and pat it over the Ivory at random. Since the light source is from the left, be sure these areas are lighter on that side.

Step 8—Using Walnut, apply vertical slashes and patches on the tree trunks, avoiding the bark-free areas. Make the brushstrokes ⅛" to ¼" long and about the width of a toothpick. Use horizontal strokes on the branches.

Step 9—Load the brush with Medium Brown and, using the same types of strokes, apply bark texture to the trees. Stop these strokes just short of the right sides. Apply a second coat of Medium Brown on the left half of each tree trunk. Lighten the upper sides of the limbs with Medium Brown.

Step 10—Load a liner brush with Ivory and touch branches of the broken tree to indicate areas that are missing bark. Use a thin wash of Medium Brown and tint these Ivory areas at random.

Step 11—Use Wedgwood Blue to make highlights on the trees, applying the color as in the previous steps and keeping it on the left edges. Apply the color a bit heavier on the trees at the right and here and there on the upper parts of the branches.

Step 12—Paint the pine needles, which flair out from little knuckle-like bumps on the branches and at there ends, as follows:

If desired, lightly sketch in a few needles, making them very fine and about ¼" to ½" long. If you have trouble painting fine lines, load a liner brush with color, flatten the bristles, and use the flattened edge rather than the point of the brush.

Paint a few needles with Black, then add some Avocado needles over them. Do not make the trees too "busy" with pine needles.

Step 13—Make very fine and mostly vertical lines of Black at random to indicate the bark patches. Do not completely outline any bark patch. Make the lines a bit wider on the left side of any bark patch that borders an Ivory area. Make a thin to medium wash of Black and use it for shadows (see the photo).

Step 14—At this point the background could be considered finished, but a nice touch is to add a vignette of some ghostly distant trees. Add these ghostly trees with a thin wash of Medium Brown. (If you wish, add these trees after the piece has been sprayed with sealer, and you will be able to wipe them off with a damp sponge if they do not please you. It may be necessary to use a stronger wash of color over the spray to keep the color from beading up.

At the same time, use a medium wash of Walnut to add some tree branches on the back of the piece. Or, use a medium wash of Medium Brown to add vague, distant tree shapes.

Step 15—Paint the eagle as outlined in the chapter, "Eagle Painting Instructions."

Step 16—Allow the piece to dry, then spray it heavily with matte sealer. Apply the spray twice, allowing ample drying time between applications.

At this point, add the vignette of trees as directed above and/or add a spider web-like veining of Black or Walnut at the lower edge as shown in the photo.

Step 17—Since this piece, with its fine details in the trees, looks better with a flat finish, spray the piece with porcelain-type sealer.

Kinzie Mold KR5

Flight of Eagles
Wedgwood Blue Marbelized Background

Step 1—Clean the greenware, then fire it to cone 04.

Step 2—Thin some Black gloss glaze with a little water and use it to pour glaze the inside of the bisque piece. Pour out the excess glaze and allow the piece to drain well. Fire the vase to cone 05.

Step 3—Avoiding the eagles, base coat the entire background with Wedgwood Blue.

Step 4—Sparingly load a ¾" Taklon shader brush with Wedgwood and tip it with Ivory. Bounce the brush straight up and down a few times on the palette to achieve a slight blend of colors. Using this same up-and-down motion and hitting the ware aggressively, stipple the colors at random over the entire background. Although it is not possible to avoid the eagles entirely, take care not to fill the details with this smack-dab color application. Also try to keep the area around the eagles light in color. Allow the piece to dry.

Step 5—Make a thin wash of Black. Referring to the photo and using the Black wash, set in the smoky-looking areas with the same up-and-down brush motion. Try to leave the areas around the eagles untouched with "islands" of Wedgwood Blue and Ivory showing here and there. Work to achieve a lacy pathway of oddly-shaped areas over the background.

Step 6—Use a heavy wash of Black to add some random craze lines at the outer edges of the sky area. To make these, use short, wiggly lines, having them unconnected and widely spaced (see the photo). Take care that you do not overdo this effect.

Step 7—Paint the eagles as outlined in the chapter, "Eagle Painting Instructions."

Step 8—Finish the piece as directed in the section, Matte, Porcelain-type Spray, and Polish.

Kinzie Mold K108

Flight of Eagles
Southwestern Background

Step 1—Clean the greenware in the usual manner. Eliminate the inside rim at the neck of the vase so the edge is plain as on a coffee cup. Fire the greenware to cone 05.

Step 2—Thin some Bean Pot Brown glaze with a little water and use it to pour glaze the bisque vase. Pour out the excess glaze and allow the piece to drain well. Fire the vase to cone 04.

Step 3—Measure up about 1¾" from the bottom of the vase and lightly place a mark at this location at 3 places on the front and back of the piece. Also place a mark on each end. Use a pencil to lightly connect the dots (the background painting will go completely around the vase).

Mark off another band, placing it about 1½" above the first one, then add a final band about 3" higher up. Do not be concerned about the narrow bands. They will be added later.

Step 4—Lightly sketch in a design of your choice on the 3" band or make a copy of the pattern and trace it on.

Step 5—Paint the top section of the vase Yellow Sand (a yellowish light brown color). Apply Ivory to the design areas and to the 1½" band. Use Cinnamon around the designs and for the bottom band.

Select a sponge with fine holes and load it with Burnt Orange. Lightly sponge this color over the Cinnamon area, work up to the edges as closely as possible. Use a brush to stipple Burnt Orange from the sponged area up to the edge of the area. Repair any overlapped colors now.

Step 6—Lightly sketch in lines for the narrow bands, placing them as shown in the photo. Paint these bands with a liner brush, making them about ⅛" wide and using Yellow Sand for the bottom one, a mixture of Cinnamon and Ivory for the next, and Cinnamon for the top one.

Step 7—Base coat the heads and tail of the eagles with Wedgwood Blue and base coat the bodies with Black.

Step 8—Paint the eagles as directed in the section "Eagle Painting Instructions."

Step 9—Spray the piece with porcelain-type sealer.

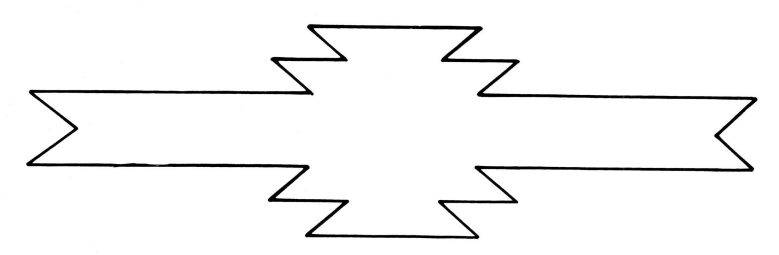

Kinzie Mold K108

Thunder in the Sky

Step 1—Clean the greenware, then fire it to cone 04.

Step 2—Thin some Black gloss glaze and pour glaze the inside of the bisque vase. Pour out the excess glaze and allow the vase to drain well. Fire the piece to cone 05.

Step 3—Avoiding the eagles, base coat the remainder of the piece with Baby Blue, using a ¾″ Taklon brush.

Step 4—Slightly thin a little Bright Blue with a few drops of water. Load the brush with the thinned color and, starting at the top, brush completely around the vase. Try to keep the strokes long and as horizontal as possible. Work quickly as possible to achieve the same effect on the back of the vase as on the front. Bring this tone down just past the tops of the wings and do not be concerned if there are any vague horizontal streaks in the color.

Step 5—Add a few drops of Bright Blue to a quarter-size puddle of White on the palette to achieve a color between Baby Blue and Bright Blue. Still using horizontal brushstrokes, start at the eagles and work out around the vase and back to the other side of the eagles. Beginning behind the lowest wing tip, apply horizontal strokes of White, allowing the color to fade away before you reach the side of the vase. Allow the piece to dry.

Step 6—Make a wash of Persimmon. Leaving the White at the feather tips, tint some of the upper White areas with this wash (see the photo). Make a very thin wash of Shocking Pink and add small amounts of it to the sky, using horizontal strokes to tint the Persimmon and White areas.

Step 7—Refer to the photo and lightly sketch in the thunderhead clouds. Avoiding the small cloud by the eagle's head, base coat all other clouds with an undiluted mixture of Black and Navy. Base coat the small cloud with a heavy wash of White.

Step 8—Tint the light cloud with thin washes of Persimmon and Burnt Orange. Highlight the dark clouds with a medium wash of Grape and brighten them with a medium wash of Purple. For the clouds facing the light source, edge them in Burnt Orange. If you wish, tint the dark parts of the clouds with a thin wash of Magenta (see the photo and refer to the section on painting clouds).

Step 9—Paint the eagles as directed in the section "Eagle Painting Instructions."

Step 10—Finish the piece, referring to the Matte, Porcelain-type Spray, and Polish section of the chapter on finishes.

Kinzie Mold K108

Fawn

Step 1—Clean the greenware, then fire it to cone 04.

Step 2—Slightly thin some Black gloss glaze and use it to pour glaze the inside of the bisque vase.

Fire the piece to cone 05.

Step 3—Base coat the entire outside of the vase with Black.

Step 4—Side brush or drybrush the entire deer with Walnut.

Step 5—Highlight the fur with Medium Brown, starting at the spine and stopping halfway down the tail, hip, stomach, tops of the legs, the side not including the stomach, tops of ears, and the forehead and snout.

Step 6—Using a ½″ shader brush and a thin wash of Burnt Orange, lightly tint the crevices, upper leg and tummy where the legs lie against the body, top of the head, forehead crease, back, cheek, and tops of the ears.

Step 7—Make a thin wash of Harvest Gold and use it for the final highlight color. Apply this wash in areas where the sun would strike the fawn such as top of the spine, hip, shoulders, tops of legs, forehead, cheek under the eye, tops of ears, and down the center of the snout to the nose. If the fur color seems too bright, tone it down by applying a thin wash of Walnut over the entire deer.

Step 8—Referring to the photo for placement, apply White inside the ears, on the eye patch, tufts of fur over the hooves, muzzle, edge of the tail, and lightly on the backs of the legs. Side brush White about ½″ wide adjacent to the tail on the fawn's bottom and lower tummy.

Step 9—Using a ⅛″ brush, side brush the dots on the body with White. Use the same brush to apply a ragged accent of White on the back of the cheek, tapering the color off and stop even with the eye patch. Accent the edge of the head to indicate the other eye.

Step 10—Apply thin washes of Harvest Gold and Bright Pink over the inside of the ear, leaving a ½″ border of White showing.

Step 11—Base coat the eye with Black. Use a thin wash of Walnut to paint an elongated "U"-shaped iris, making it wider toward the back of the head and tapering off toward the front. Allow the eye to dry. Make a thin wash of Medium Brown and highlight the iris at the 8 o'clock position. If the eye color is too bright, go over the entire eye with a thin wash of Black.

Using a liner brush and the Black wash, make a broad shadow under the top lid and across the eyeball. Also make a line around the bottom lid and shade the back half of the iris.

Step 12—Touch up the hooves with Black and darken the dew claw. Make a thin wash of Black and shadow all crevices such as the leg, hip, around the head, between the tail, and, starting at the head and stopping halfway out, inside the ears. Also accent the tear duct.

Step 13—Use undiluted White for the highlight of the eye. Use a thin wash of White to highlight the nose.

Step 14—Sign the piece, then spray it with 2 coats of matte sealer, allowing drying time between coats. Allow the vase to stand overnight, then spray it with porcelain-type sealer. Apply brush-on gloss sealer to the eye.

Kinzie Mold K110

Wolf Woman

Step 1—Clean the greenware, then fire it to cone 04.

Step 2—Glaze the inside with Antique Brown.

BACKGROUND

Step 1—Base coat the background areas with Ivory, using a ¾″ brush.

Step 2—Sparingly load a brush with Ivory and tip the corner of it in Medium Brown. With the brush loaded in this way, smack-dab the background, keeping the color lighter near the top half of the piece. Allow the piece to dry. Make a medium thin wash of Medium Brown. Sparingly load the ¾″ brush with this wash and darken the bottom of the vase at an angle from the right side near the wolf's ear down to the woman's hand. Be sure the division line between the colors is vague.

INDIAN WOMAN

Step 1—Base coat the skin areas with Native Flesh and allow them to dry. Make a thin wash of Burnt Orange. Lightly load a brush with this wash and tint the skin, being sure there are no brush marks. Apply a thin wash of Walnut for a tanned skin tone. Repeat the Walnut applications, allowing drying time between them until the desired flesh tone is achieved.

Step 2—Apply a very thin wash of Ivory to the fingernails. Block in the eyes with undiluted Ivory.

Step 3—Apply the cheek color with the "no fail" cheek method (see Indian Girl and Pony, Step 10).

Step 4—Make a medium wash of Medium Brown. Use this wash for the irises of the eyes, allowing the edges of the irises to go under the top and bottom lids. Allow the eyes to dry. Using a very thin wash of Walnut, sparingly load a detail brush or a ⅛″ shader and tint the top halves of the irises. Add Black pupils and allow the piece to dry.

Strengthen the Walnut wash with a touch or two of undiluted color. Use fine lines of this color to outline the edges of the irises. Add a drop of Black to the wash and add a thin shadow across the upper half of each eye. Use this same wash to shadow the upper lids, inside the ear, the nostrils, the curl crevice of the nose, in between the fingers, around the nails, and inside the hollow of her hand.

Step 5—Place a small drop of Bright Red on the palette. Mix a little Walnut into the Bright Red to tone it down. Make a thin wash of the mixture and apply it to the lips. Allow the lips to dry. Use a fine line of a heavy Black wash to separate the lips. Also use this wash to outline the eyelids on the skin next to the eyes and to add a few eyelashes (if desired, sketch in a few lashes with a pencil to check the placement).

Step 6—Darken a bit of Walnut with some Black and add the eyebrows, painting 1 hair at a time with a liner or detail brush.

Step 7—Base coat the feather with Ivory. Tint the feather, beginning at the outside and working inward about ⅘ of the way at the same angle as the detail crevices, with a thin wash of Harvest Gold. Repeat this step with Medium Brown, stopping the strokes about halfway on the Harvest Gold areas. Apply a narrow, ragged edge, using a medium/thin wash of Black and a ¼″ shader brush. Outline both sides of the quill. Paint the bead at the end of the feather and the 2 hairs coming from it with Black.

Step 8—Load a brush with White and slide the side of it down the center of the feather quill. Make the bead Turquoise and the horsehairs Medium Brown. Apply a black/brown mixture of Black and Walnut to the hair.

WOLF

Step 1—Base coat the wolf with Black.

Step 2—Lightly drybrush all areas that are to be White such as inside the ears, sides of the muzzle, under the eyes, the primary bumps on the brow, and over the eyes. Also add sketchy lines against the nose, making them longer in the center of the snout, on the border fur around the face, on the throat, and across the bottom of the cheek.

Step 3—Side brush the backs of the ears with Walnut. Also side brush Walnut across the forehead and down the top of the snout. Leave a narrow area of Black showing.

Step 4—Referring to the photo, apply "v"-shaped bands, using White, Black, a wide band of Walnut, and a narrow band of Black on the cheeks. On the throat apply bands of White, a broad band of Walnut, very narrow bands of Black and White, and end with a broad band of Black under the muzzle to represent a shadow.

Step 5—Dot the cheeks and throat at random with Medium Brown over the Walnut areas. Make a thin wash of Medium Brown and apply over the white on the front of the chin, mustache area, and slightly at the back of the muzzle area.

Step 6—Dilute a drop of Bright Pink into a thin wash. Apply this wash inside the ears, beginning at the base. Maintain a loose triangle shape in each ear and stop about ½″ from the edge of each one. Add a very little Bright Pink over the back of the muzzle area where it touches the cheeks. Apply a thin wash of Harvest Gold over the pink wash in the ears.

Kinzie Mold K109

Step 7—Block in the eyes with White and allow them to dry. Coat the eye areas with a thin wash of Harvest Gold. Add the pupils, having the tops go under the eyelids with only a sliver of iris showing in each eye.

Step 8—Make a thin wash of Black and apply to areas where you wish to accent the detail. Wipe back the color with a damp cloth, leaving Black in the detail crevices. In this way accent inside the ears, the muzzle, eye patches, and any other areas as desired.

Step 9—Outline the eyes with Black, having the lines raggedy on the fur sides. Outline the mouth opening and add a narrow border pattern of Black about 1/8" from the edges of the ears. Apply Black to the nose to repair the shape if necessary.

Step 10—Use a thin wash of Black to shadow the top half of each eye, tapering these shadows to the corners. Highlight the wolf's and the woman's eyes with dots of White, placing the dot in the same relative position in each eye.

FINISHING TOUCHES

Step 1—Side brush White to add accents over the inside of the wolf's ears, on its muzzle, the woman's feather, and elsewhere as desired. Side brush Walnut over the raised strands of the woman's hair.

Step 2—Spray the piece with 2 coats of matte sealer, allowing drying time between them. Allow the piece to dry overnight, then spray porcelain-type sealer on the woman and the wolf. Allow the piece to dry and polish the background as directed in the section on finishes. Apply gloss sealer to the eyes.

Mother and Baby Wolves

Step 1—Clean the greenware, then fire it to cone 04.

Step 2—Thin some Black gloss glaze and pour glaze the inside of the bisque piece.

Fire the jug to cone 05.

Step 3—Using a ¾" brush, base coat the entire outside of the jug with Black water-base stain. Thin some Walnut with water. Sparingly load the same brush and stipple the thinned color over the background.

Step 4—Referring to the photo as you work, set in the major white areas with undiluted White and the side brushing technique. Use brushes suited to the sizes of the areas being covered. Apply the White to such areas as muzzles, chins, under throats, cheeks, feet, backs of legs, fronts of rear legs, eye patches, stomach and chest of the baby, the tip of the mother's tail, and the teeth. Lightly apply a little White to the mother's stomach.

Step 5—For the mother's hip and shoulder that go around to the back of the jug, apply ragged horseshoe shapes of White, Black, and Walnut. Apply Medium Brown over the Walnut areas.

Step 6—Randomly apply Walnut to the fur details in the Black areas. Make a medium wash of Walnut and paint the insides of the baby's back legs to contrast with the stomach. Add a drop or 2 of Walnut to the wash and apply to all claws.

Step 7—Make a medium/thin wash of Medium Brown. Using a ⅛" shader brush on its edge, tint the crevices between the toes. Also tint a very small area at the front of each chin and add a bit of shadow around the noses. Also apply the Medium Brown wash to the White areas to set them off from the dark areas.

Step 8—Have a dampened soft cloth near at hand. Flood the baby's bib and chest with the Medium Brown wash and quickly wipe back, leaving the dark color only in the crevices. Do the same with the mother's cheek, throat, and to the White areas of her tail.

Step 9—Apply a thin wash of Bright Pink to the baby's stomach and immediately wipe back. Place pink in the ears, leaving a clean border in each. Apply a very light touch of the pink wash on the cheek fur and along the lower eyelids. Mix Walnut into the wash and apply to the pads of the baby's feet.

Step 10—Base coat the mother's eye with White. Make a thin wash of Harvest Gold and tint the eye and inside the ears over the pink wash. Paint a Black pupil in the eye, setting it toward the nose. Highlight the eye with White.

Step 11—Apply a thin wash of Black to all crevices such as between the toes, both sides of the legs and hips, and in separations of the fur areas. Shadow the ears where they connect to the head.

Step 12—Slightly thin some Black and use a liner or detail brush to outline the eyes. Outline the lower lips, having the line ragged toward the fur. Outline the claws.

Step 13—Sign the jug and allow it to dry. Spray the piece with 2 coats of matte sealer and allow it to dry overnight. Spray the piece with porcelain-type sealer to dull the shine. Apply gloss sealer to the mother's eye.

Kinzie Mold K111

Wolves

Step 1—Clean the greenware box and lid.

Step 2—Apply 1 coat of Off White texture glaze to the outside of the box, stopping at the upper rim. Allow the piece to dry. Sponge 2 coats of the texture glaze over the same areas, allowing drying time between coats. Clean off any glaze that may be on the top lip of the box.

Fire the box and the lid to cone 04.

Step 3—Following the manufacturer's directions, glaze the inside of the box including the rim and the inside of the lid.

Place the lid upside down in the kiln to avoid stilt marks and fire it and the box to the recommended temperature.

Step 4—Base coat the background area of the lid and the bottom of the box with Ivory stain. Avoiding the flower petals, base coat the remainder of the embossed lid design with Black. Allow the pieces to dry.

Step 5—Make a thin wash of Medium Brown. Use a sponge to lightly pat a narrow border of the thinned color on the edge of the lid. Also pat the color on the unglazed areas on the underside of the lid. Pat a border of the thinned Medium Brown around the top and bottom of the box sides, leaving the center area free of this color. Set the lid on the box to make sure the sponged borders match. Adjust as necessary.

Step 6—Side brush the embossed ground area and the stump with Walnut. Side brush Medium Brown here and there over the ground. Apply Avocado on random areas of the ground and paint lines of the same color over the grasses and leaves. Highlight a few areas with Lime.

Step 7—Make a medium wash of White. Sparingly load a ¼" shader brush with the wash. Holding the brush upright at the edge of the large tree, pull curved strokes across the trunk. Allow these strokes to overlap as you work up the tree, keeping the lightest area at the right edge. Repeat these strokes again. Add more White to the wash and add shorter strokes across the tree at random.

Make a medium/heavy wash of Black and add a few streaks and dots on the tree to give the effect of birch bark.

Step 8—Apply a coat of Ivory to all wood areas without bark and allow them to dry. Apply a thin wash of Harvest Gold to these same areas. Apply a thin wash of Medium Brown, leaving the tops and centers of these areas open and fairly free of color.

Step 9—Side brush the thin tree with Wedgwood Blue and add a few hit-or-miss strokes to the right side of the stump. Paint the small twig in the foreground in the same way.

Step 10—Referring to the photo, apply White to all areas on the wolves that are to be light such as muzzles, lower cheeks and edges up to the ears, and the tip and edge of the mother's tail. Also make a "U" shape on the mother's rear leg, an upside down "U" shape on the back of her neck (like a collar), and on any other areas that you wish to be bright in tone.

Step 11—Side brush Walnut over the Black areas. Highlight and warm edges of the Walnut areas with Medium Brown.

Step 12—Apply undiluted Pink to the flower petals and make the centers Harvest Gold. Make a thin wash of Pink and pat vague, oddly-shaped patches on the right side of the birch tree. Repeat with a thin wash of Harvest Gold. Add a wash of Pink inside the wolves' ears, leaving the edges clean.

Step 13—Base coat the wolves' eyes and the butterfly and stones with Ivory.

Flood the eyes with a wash of Harvest Gold. Coat the butterfly and a few grasses and leaves with this color.

Add Black pupils to the eyes and repair the nose colors as needed. Slightly thin a little Black and add fine lines to everything but the flower petals. Make sure to add fine lines on the legs, tail, and faces, taking care not to make the eyes smaller.

Step 14—Make a thin wash of Black and shadow under the mother and cub, the bottom of the thin tree, and the left sides of all trees. Add a shadow on the ground of the foreground twig and divide the butterfly wings.

Set the lid aside while you finish the box sides.

Step 15—Lightly sketch 2 elongated ovals on the box, placing one on each side.

Cut or tear long ½"-wide strips of paper towel. Place a paper strip across a puddle of white glue. Use your fingers to work the glue into the towel as you twist and turn it once or twice. Set this glued strip on a pencil line and work it around one oval. Press and smooth the paper towel strip away from the "hole." Repeat for the other oval.

Kinzie Molds K1G and K1

Step 16—Make a broken twig by cutting or tearing a 2″ strip of paper towel. Coat one side of the strip with glue. Fold the strip in half lengthwise; glue sides together. Apply glue to one side of the folded strip. Starting at one end, tightly roll the strip, keeping the folded edge neat. When the "twig" is of the desired thickness, tear off the excess and pull open the ragged edge. Add a thin coat of glue on the box side where you wish to place the twig. Set the twisted paper on the glue and push it down with your fingers to secure it in place.

Allow the box to dry for about 8 hours or overnight.

Step 17—Apply a thin wash of Harvest Gold to the "holes" and to the ends of the applied branch. Make a thin wash of Medium Brown. Tap this color on the end of the twig and streak it horizontally across the knotholes.

Base coat the outsides of the applied knotholes and the twig with Black. Go over the Black with Walnut and Medium Brown and touch the turned-up edges with a little White.

Add some fine lines of Black around the twig as shown in the photo.

Foxes and Butterfly

Step 1—Clean the greenware, then fire it to cone 04.

Step 2—Thinking of the piece as a clock face and leaving a ragged edge, base coat the sky area between the 10 o'clock and 2 o'clock positions.

Step 3—Base coat all trees, the ground, and the leaves with Black. Use an old, "toothy" ¼" brush to stipple Black in an up-and-down motion around the fox and up to the Ivory sky area. Try to have this stippled color resemble foliage.

Load a brush with lightly thinned Dark Green, then pick up a little Light Blue. Stab the brush up and down on the palette to begin blending the colors. With the brush loaded and conditioned in this way, stipple the Black foliage area. Pay special attention to the grasses.

Step 4—Side brush the grasses under the foxes with Avocado.

Step 5—Side brush White on the birch tree. Paint the bare, bark-free areas of the leaning tree and the top of the broken stump with Ivory. Apply a thin wash of Harvest Gold here and there on the White and Ivory areas of the trees.

Step 6—Using a liner or detail brush, paint the leaves with Lime. Highlight some of the foreground grasses with the same color. If desired, paint a few lines for leaves in the background with Black.

Step 7—Sparingly load a ¼" Taklon brush with Walnut and slide the side of the brush along the bark of the stump and the leaning trees. Use Medium Brown to highlight the center of the stump and the top half of the leaning tree.

Thin a bit of Medium Brown to a wash and tint a few wedge shapes here and there on the birch tree, being sure to follow the crevices. Repeat this with a thin wash of Black. Also darken the "hole" on the tree.

Step 8—Apply White to the rocks, the flowers including their centers, and the butterfly. Allow the piece to dry. Paint the flower centers and the butterfly Harvest Gold. Mix a gray from a little Black and White and use it to apply shadows to the rocks. Paint the foreground and the broken stick Gray.

Step 9—Base coat the foxes with Ivory, covering any colors that may have overlapped onto the fur.

Step 10—Apply full strength White to the insides of the ears, the end of the mother's tail, and the cheek edges of both foxes. Also apply White to the cub's tummy and inner lower leg and to the mother's neck, chest, and neck line.

Step 11—Make a thin wash of Harvest Gold and apply it so it overlaps the white edge of the tail where the red orange of the fur will connect. Lightly tint the insides of the ears with this wash, leaving their outer edges white.

Step 12—Using a medium wash of Burnt Orange and taking care not to overload the brush, paint the remainder of the fur areas. As you bring this color up to the white areas, try to achieve ragged edges in the direction that the fur lies. Apply a thin wash of Pink over the Harvest Gold inside the ears. Allow the piece to dry.

Step 13—Apply Black to the back of the ears. Do not end with straight lines where they join the heads, but with a ragged, arced bow in the center of each ear. Apply Black to the feet and lower legs. Apply the Black about halfway up the cub's legs, forming a

point of fine lines on each one. Paint the noses and mouth lines Black and add the small patches on the muzzles (see the photo). Paint long Black "hairs" in the division between the white of the mother's tail and the Burnt Orange area.

Step 14—Paint the eyes Harvest Gold and allow them to dry. Add a tall oval of Black to each eye as a pupil and highlight with a dot of White in the upper left. Outline the eyes with Black, making ragged edges on the fur sides. If you end up with a broad line, correct it with Burnt Orange.

Step 15—Use a heavy wash of Black to add the cast shadow on the ground from the foreground branch. Load a ⅛" Taklon brush with Black and shade the crevices between the mother's tail and hip. Shadow all remaining crevices such as around the heads, both sides of the legs, necklines, and the mother's shoulders. Very lightly and sparingly shade the "frown" lines, the sides of the muzzles, the snouts, and the eyebrow areas. Underline the rocks with fine lines and, if necessary, separate the flower petals and leaves. Shadow the insides of the ears, making the shadows narrow and have them follow the deepest areas inside the ears. Carefully apply fine hair lines between the cub's white cheek fur and the Burnt Orange areas. Lightly accent the eyebrows.

Step 16—Make a thin wash of 2 drops of Bright Red. Sparingly load a ½" shader brush with the wash. Set the brush in the crevice along the mother's tail and, pulling the brush as the fur lies, paint a "U" shape with a ragged edge. Tint all Burnt Orange areas next to the White ones. Tint the backs and sides of both foxes in the same way, avoiding any areas where the light might strike. Allow the piece to dry.

Kinzie Mold K1G

Step 17—Make a thin wash of Black. Working quickly and on a small area at a time, cover the mother's tail. Cover your finger with a single layer of damp cloth and wipe off the fur to clear the raised areas and leave the wash in the crevices. Continue in this way, taking care that you do not go over the eyes and clean the white areas thoroughly.

Step 18—Sign the piece, then spray it with 2 coats of matte sealer. Allow the piece to dry overnight, then spray it with porcelain-type sealer.

To display the finished piece, hang it as a picture or set it on a small gold tripod.

Mouse Stone

Step 1—If you wish to make the piece into a clock, ask that it be kept damp when you order the greenware. Set the clockworks on the damp greenware and draw around it with a pencil. Using a cleaning tool or a sharp knife, cut through the greenware along the traced line. Check to see that the clock fits loosely into the hole to allow for shrinkage that will take place when the piece is fired.

Clean the greenware and fire it to cone 05. Check to see that the clock fits into the hole. Use sandpaper to enlarge the hole as necessary.

Step 2—Using a ¾″ shader brush, base coat the stone with Black. Clean the brush and sparingly load it with slightly thinned Walnut. Use an aggressive, up-and-down stippling motion to pounce color over the rock surface. Do not completely cover all of the Black base coat. Load the brush with Medium Brown and tip it with White. Smack dab these colors on the rock, allowing the brushstrokes to overlap

and be sure the stone is dark to contrast with the mouse.

Step 3—Base coat the mouse with Gray. Paint the inside of the ears, around the eyes, and the muzzle with White. Allow the piece to dry. Thin some Bright Pink and apply it to the nose. Thin the color further and tint the insides of the ears, toes, and tail. Lightly "dust" this wash over the cheek and on the edge of the white muzzle.

Step 4—Paint the bedding grass Bright Yellow. Make a thin wash of Medium Brown and apply fine lines in the crevices of the bedding. Use a thin wash of Bright Yellow to tint over the pink in the ears, stopping just beyond the pink areas.

Check to be sure the wall behind the mouse is Black and, if not, touch up as necessary.

Step 5—Use a detail brush to paint the pupil of the mouse's eye with full strength Medium Brown. Following the

contour of the bottom lid, making an elongated "U" shape, highlight the eye with a comma stroke of White. Outline the eye and the tear duct with a fine line of Black.

Step 6—Outline the entire mouse with fine lines of Black, including its toes and tail. Thin the Black with a little water and add fine lines to the tail. Also use fine lines to divide the layers of bedding grass.

Step 7—Make fine, sketchy Black outlines around the eye patches and add the mouth line. Thin the Black to a smoky tone and paint a shadow on the stone of the mouse's chin and tail. Also add a shadow under the grass.

Step 8—Apply a thin wash of Black to the entire mouse. Immediately cover your finger with a damp cloth and wipe the mouse, so the Black remains only in the crevices.

Step 9—Allow the piece to dry, then finish it with matte spray and polish as directed in the section on finishes.

Swiss Cheese Mouse

Step 1—Clean and prepare the piece as for the preceding project, then fire it to cone 05.

Step 2—Avoiding the mouse, base coat the remainder of the piece with Pale Yellow.

Step 3—Use a pencil to very lightly sketch cheese "holes" over the entire background. Make a thin wash of Harvest Gold and apply to each outlined hole. Prepare a thin wash of

Medium Brown. Load a ⅛″ shader brush with this wash and shade the upper part of each hole with "C" strokes.

Step 4—Using the same washes as in the previous step, pat them at random inside the walls of the mouse hole. Apply a wash of Medium Brown to the crevices of the straw bedding. Thin a drop of Avocado into a thin wash and pat it at random over the grasses.

Step 5—Complete the mouse as directed in the previous project.

Step 6—Shadow the layer effect around the sides of the piece, using a ⅛″ brush and a thin wash of Medium Brown.

Step 7—Spray the piece with 2 coats of matte sealer and allow it to dry overnight. Spray the piece again, this time with porcelain-type sealer.

Kinzie Mold K39

Kinzie Mold K39

Onyx Eagle Box

Step 1—Clean the greenware, then fire the box with the lid in place to cone 04.

Step 2—Pour glaze the insides of the box and lid with Black gloss glaze. Use a brush to apply glaze to the lip of the box and lid.

Place the pieces into the kiln with the lid face down on the shelf to avoid stilt marks and the box separate. Fire to cone 06.

Step 3—Base coat the bisque areas of the box and the background areas of the lid with Black. Smack dab the same areas with Navy and White. Be sure the brush is moist and pounce it straight up and down on a tile to begin to blend the Navy and White. Use the same up-and-down motion to apply the colors to the background. Allow the colors to slightly overlap the eagle, but do not let them fill in the detail crevices.

Step 4—Base coat the eagle's feathers with Wedgwood Blue and its beak with Ivory.

Step 5—Referring to the section of side brushing, side brush the eagle's feathers with White.

Side brush the eagle so the Whitest areas are the top of the head and on the lower cheek area.

Step 6—Thin some Harvest Gold to a very thin wash and apply it to the eye. Immediately remove the color from the eye from the 5 o'clock to the 7 o'clock position, using a small damp brush. Add enough Gold to the wash to make medium wash. Use this color to darken the upper third of the eye.

Step 7—Apply a medium wash of Harvest Gold to the beak, then shadow the bottom with a thin wash of Medium Brown. Use a #2 shader brush to dampen the upper edge, blending the color away into the beak. Make a thin wash of Walnut and paint lines around the beak where it touches the feathers. Also use this wash to shade the nose indention and the crevice between sections of the beak. Slightly thin some Black and add a fine line between the beak sections. Thin a bit of Black to a thin wash and tint the nostril.

Step 8—Paint the raised ring around the eye Gold. Make a thin wash of Burnt Orange and tint this border area. Also tint the top half of the eye to slightly darken it. Allow the piece to dry, then add a Black pupil. Make the pupil slightly off center and toward the upper forward part of the eye. Allow the pupil to dry, then add a highlight between the 10 and 11 o'clock locations.

Step 9—Prepare a very thin wash of Purple and have at hand a damp cloth. Shade only the feathers with this wash as follows: Apply the color, then immediately wipe the area with the damp cloth over your finger. In this way shade over the eye, from the beak outward, on the throat, and at random over the edges of the feathers.

Allow the piece to dry. Make a very thin wash of Harvest Gold and lightly apply to the feathers where the sun would strike them. Immediately wipe off the wash to leave only a glow of color.

Step 10—Use a heavy wash of Black and outline the eye. Apply a slightly wider line in the crevice at the top of the eye and allow it to taper off toward the back of the head.

Step 11—Spray the lid and the stain areas of the box with 2 coats of matte sealer. Remove any spray that may be on the glaze areas with 000 or 0000 steel wool.

Broken Gold

Step 1—Prepare the greenware as directed in Steps 1 and 2 of the previous project. Base coat the background areas with Black. Complete the eagle as directed in the previous project, then spray the eagle with sealer.

Step 2—Apply Gold foil to the background areas as follows:

Lay several layers of newspapers on the work surface and replace them as they become sticky.

Shake a spray can of glue, then spray the back of the foil. Allow the glue on the foil to become tacky. Apply a small, 1″ or 2″ by ½″ piece of foil neatly at the edges of the eagle, pressing it down and rubbing it with your fingers or with a tongue depressor. Hold one edge of the foil and tear off the remainder. (The glue acts as a bonding agent for the gold color. When you tear off the remainder, it will look like a piece of cellophane.) In this way cover the entire background of the lid and the box sides with irregular-shaped pieces of metallic gold bits of color.

Check with your local studio or art suppliers for the gold foil. Do not use iron-on or heat release foil. The product used for this project can be obtained from Sax Arts & Crafts, 2405 S. Calhoun Rd., New Berlin, WI 53151, phone 1-800-558-6696.

Kinzie Molds K1H and K1